Contents

Home FUN booklet

Melissa Owen

Animals

jellyfish

boat

1 Write and draw lines.

Zoo

....

....

....

....

....

....

....

....

2 Read and complete the descriptions.
What animal is it?

~~green~~   short legs   ~~jump~~   brown   black and white   long tail
legs   milk   eggs   green brown and red   ~~long legs~~   run

It's .... green ....
It has .... long legs ....
It can .... jump ....
It's a .... frog ....

It's ....
It has a ....
It can ....
It's a ....

It's ....
It has four ....
It can make ....
It's a ....

It's ....
It has two ....
It can give you ....
It's a ....

3 Draw and colour an animal. Write about your animal.

My animal is a/an

....

It is ....

It has ....

....

It can ....

....

4 Say a letter of the alphabet and say an animal.

B – bird, bee!

J – jellyfish!

5 Can you find the animals?

polarbearsnakecrocodilechickenbirdjellyfishfrogdonkeygiraffefishtigerelephant

abc ✓

How do you spell the words?

_ _ _ _ _ _ _   _ _ _ _ _ _ _ _ _

3

The body and face

1 Colour the words. Write.

t <u>e e</u> t <u>h</u>

_ _ m

e _ _

_ _ e

e	a	r	l	x	h	a	n	d	o
z	z	s	h	m	t	a	r	m	q
c	f	e	i	a	r	s	t	i	b
g	l	e	y	e	h	g	w	r	d
s	i	d	f	a	c	e	f	e	n
a	d	z	i	e	e	l	e	f	o
t	e	e	t	h	t	p	e	m	s
o	l	e	d	m	o	u	t	h	e

h _ _ _

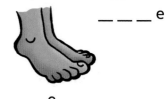

_ o _ _ _

_ _ _ e

_ _ c _

_ e _ _

2 Read and write.

brown					

brown big small long green black
short blonde red white

4

3 Read and draw the monster. Colour.

I've got long red hair.
I've got three small eyes. My eyes are green.
I've got a big, purple nose.
I've got a big mouth with five small teeth.
My body is big.
I have five arms – two are long and three are very long.
I have three legs – they look like pineapples!

4 Draw your monster. Write.

My monster!	
hair	
eyes	
nose	
mouth	
teeth	
ears	
arms	
body	
legs	

Tell your family about your monster.

We say: I've got brown hair.
Not: I've got a brown hair.

Clothes

1 **Draw lines to match.**

skirt   bag   trousers   baseball cap   jacket   glasses

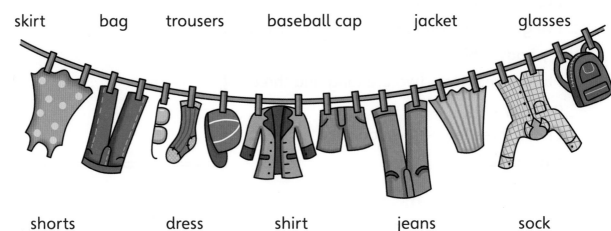

shorts   dress   shirt   jeans   sock

2 **Find and colour clothes for Anna.**

The end!

table	T-shirt	hat	shorts	bag
grandmother	boots	tree	monster	horse
happy	glasses	jeans	football	giraffe
chair	cow	skirt	car	kite
tomato	socks	shirt	beach	bike
dress	trousers	colour	brown	pink

ANNA

Start

3 **Draw and colour.**

   1 The green jeans are next to the white hat.

   2 Draw two blue socks next to the jeans.

   3 The purple jacket is next to the trousers.

   4 The green shirt is under the baseball cap.

   5 Draw some red shorts between the shirt and the dress.

4 Draw your favourite clothes. Write.

This is me. I'm wearing my ....
....
....
I like them because ....
....

5 Find a photo of your mum or dad. What are they wearing?

This is my ....
He / She is wearing ....
He / She has got ....
....
....

6 *Fun at home* In your house, what clothes can you see? Put a note on five different clothes in your room.

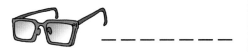

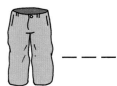

How do you spell the words?

_ _ _ _ _ _ _ _ _   _ _ _ _ _ _ _

Colours

1 Write the colours.

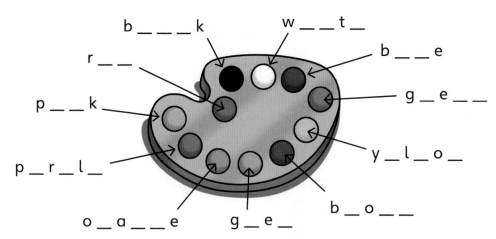

b _ _ _ k

w _ _ t _

r _ _

b _ _ e

p _ _ k

g _ e _ _

p _ r _ l _

y _ l _ o _

o _ a _ _ e

g _ e _

b _ o _ _

2 Decide colours. Colour the numbers.

colour 1 = ...

colour 4 = ...

colour 7 = ...

colour 2 = ...

colour 5 = ...

colour 3 = ...

colour 6 = ...

3 Write and colour.

1

.... + ... = ...purple......

2

.... + ... = ...

3

.... + ... = ...

4

.... + ... = ...

4 Choose three colours. Write your favourite things.

Example:
.............the sea.............
..........mummy's eyes..........
..........my new jeans..........

....
....
....

Tell your family about the colour of your favourite things.

9

Family and friends

1 Are they male or female? Write the words in the table.

~~brother~~ grandfather mother sister grandma dad ~~cousin~~ father parent grandpa classmate grandparent mum grandmother

brother		cousin

2 Draw lines. Write the words.

me grandmother mother ~~father~~ sister grandfather brother

Lucy   May   Nick

....mother....

....

....

....father.... ....

Alex   Dan   Grace   Bill

This is my family! My dad's name is Nick and he likes taking photos. My mum is Grace and she loves the colour purple. My baby brother Dan loves frogs!
My sister Lucy loves football and she plays every day. My grandpa's name is Bill and my grandma's name is May. They like walking in the park. I'm Alex and I like climbing trees! Oh and I forgot! Our cat is Tom and he loves eating our shoes!

3 **Make your family tree. Write about your family.**

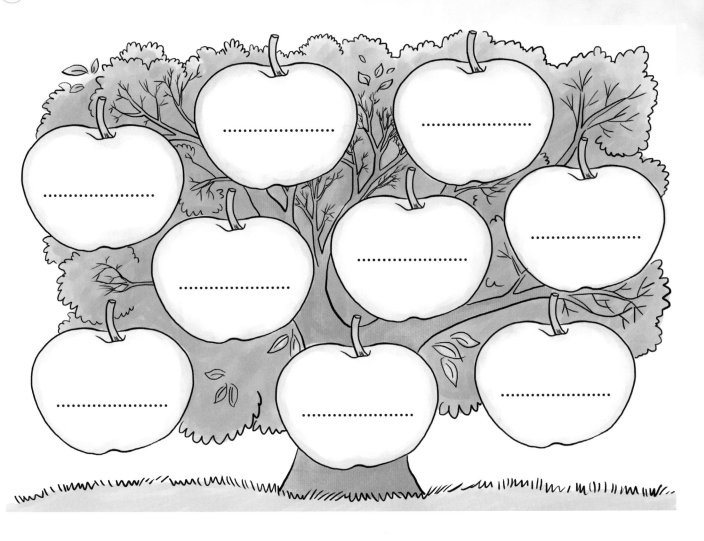

This is my family tree. My mum's name is .... and she loves
.... My dad is .... and he likes ....
My grandparents' names are .... and .... They
like .... I have / haven't got ....

abc ✓

How do you spell the word?

_ _ _ _ _ _

Food and drink

1 Find fruit and vegetables. Write the words in the correct group.

Fruit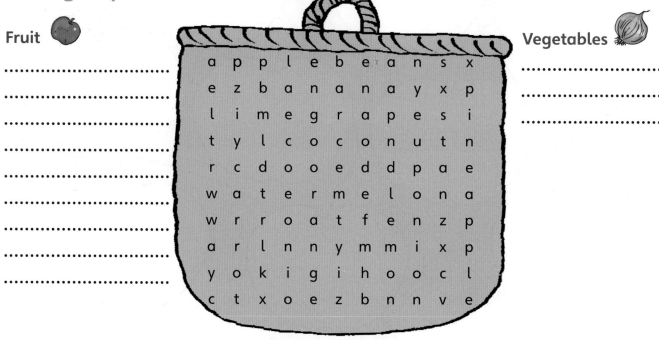

....
....
....
....
....
....
....
....
....

a	p	p	l	e	b	e	a	n	s	x
e	z	b	a	n	a	n	a	y	x	p
l	i	m	e	g	r	a	p	e	s	i
t	y	l	c	o	c	o	n	u	t	n
r	c	d	o	o	e	d	d	p	a	e
w	a	t	e	r	m	e	l	o	n	a
w	r	r	o	a	t	f	e	n	z	p
a	r	l	n	n	y	m	m	i	x	p
y	o	k	i	g	i	h	o	o	c	l
c	t	x	o	e	z	b	n	n	v	e

Vegetables
....
....
....

2 Complete the menu.

Today's menu

ch _ c _ e _
and r _ _ _ e

t _ _ _ at _ _ _ s
and _ g _ s

j _ i _ e

wat e r

s _ us _ g _ _ _

ch _ co _ _ _ t _
c _ k _

mi _ _ _

b u r g e r
and c _ _ _ _ s

p _ z _ a

f _ s _ and
po _ at _ _ s

i _ ecr _ a _

h _ t
ch _ c _ l _ t _

3 Unscramble the words.

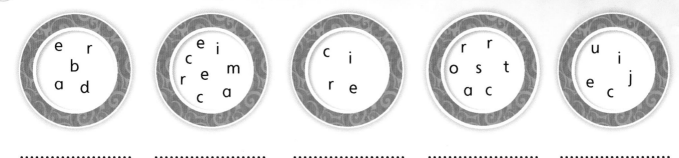

e r b a d .... c e i r e m c a .... c i r e .... r r o s t a c .... u i e j c ....

n i o n o .... k c n e i h c .... g e g s .... c e o l c a h t o e k c a ....

4 Write about you.

For breakfast

🙂🙂 I love	🙂 I like	☹ I don't like

For lunch

🙂🙂 I love	🙂 I like	☹ I don't like

For dinner

🙂🙂 I love	🙂 I like	☹ I don't like

5 *Fun at home* Make a juice drink. Write the fruit in your drink.

My drink has got:

....
....
....
....

The home

1 Write and draw lines.

d e b
b _e_ _d_

g u r
r _ _ _

s k e d
d _ _ _

m p a l
l _ _ _

r i r o m r
m _ _ r _ _

c a h m r i r a
a _ _ c _ _ i _

v o i n t l e e s i
t _ _ _ v _ s _ r

b r d u p a o c
c _ p _ _ a _ _

s e o k o b a c
b _ _ k _ a _ _

2 Write the names. What can you see?

Room: .....bathroom.....
There is a
.....mirror.....
There is a
....

Room: ....
There is a
....
There is a
....

Room: ....
There is a
....
There is a
....

Room: ....
There is a
....
There is an
....

Room: ....
There is a
....
There are
....

Place: ....
There is a
....
There are
....

14

3 Draw your bedroom. Draw lines.

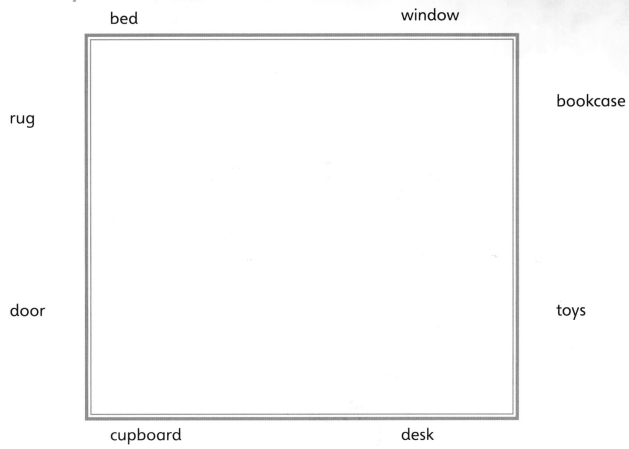

bed   window

rug   bookcase

door   toys

cupboard   desk

4 *Fun at home* Label a room in your house. You need stickers and a pen. Tell your family.

This is a chair

chair

abc ✓

How do you spell the word?

_ _ _ _ _ _

School

1 **Look. Read and colour.**

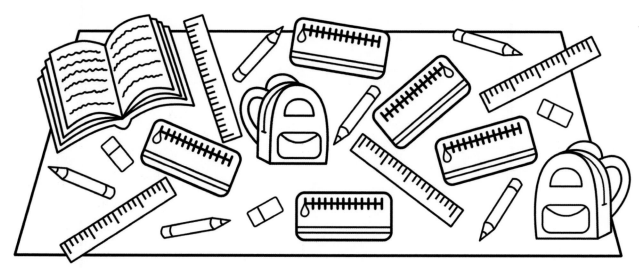

Can you find...?

1 1 book. Colour it yellow.

2 2 school bags. Colour them brown.

3 3 erasers. Colour them blue.

4 4 rulers. Colour them orange.

5 5 pencil cases. Colour them pin

6 6 pencils. Colour them green.

2 **Can you find the school words?**

posterplaygroundpagecrayonsenglishbookteacherglassescasedesk

3 **Read and draw.**

Draw a whiteboard.

Draw a brown desk under the whiteboard.

There's a teacher next to the desk.

There's a red pencil case under the desk.

There's an English book in the teacher's hand!

4 Draw your classroom. Write what you can see.

[blank drawing box]

↑
chair

5 Look at Grace's schoolbag.

In my bag I've got a book, a ruler, two pencils, a banana, an apple and juice.

What's in *your* schoolbag? Tell your family!

Sports

(1) **Read and match. Draw lines.**

ten   ball
basket   ming
badmin   nis
table   ey
swim   ball
hock   tennis
base   ton

(2) **Match.**

kick   hit   catch   throw   bounce

Read and write.

Basketball
You can
b............ ,
th.......... and
c.......... the ball.

Hockey
You can h...........
the ball with a
st..........k .

Tennis
You can b...........
and h..........
the ball with a
r...........t .

Football
You can k...........
and t.......... the
ball.

18

3 Complete the table with sports.

Tell your family.

I love fishing. I don't like basketball.

4 *Fun at home* Play with your family. Mime and draw.

Key:

⬜ = mime

☁ = draw

3 bounce a ball	4 catch a ball	11 play tennis	12 run	Finish
2 go to the beach	5 play hockey	10 hockey stick	13 play badminton	18 table tennis bat
1 play baseball	6 skateboard	9 fly	14 tennis racket	17 throw a ball
⬆ Start	7 jump 10 times	8 ride a horse	15 play basketball	16 swim in the sea

Toys

1 Circle the toys. Write.

..........doll..........

....

b	a	l	l	j	k	n	t	i	y
e	z	y	r	o	b	o	t	o	u
f	h	k	m	m	o	s	e	c	l
k	i	t	e	u	a	l	i	e	n
t	y	e	w	q	t	f	x	p	d
a	f	o	o	t	b	a	l	l	o
s	c	o	m	p	u	t	e	r	l
x	w	b	m	o	t	y	i	p	l

....

....

....

2 Read. Colour. Write.

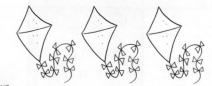

One green ....computer............ .
Two pink ....
Three orange ....
Four blue ....
Five red ....

3 Count the toys. Colour and write.

more than ten					toy	video
10						
9						
8						
7						
6						
5						
4	〰〰					
3	〰〰					
2	〰〰					
1	〰〰					
	dolls	robots	balls	kites	toy cars	video games

.........four.........dolls

.....................robots

.......................balls

....

....

....

4 Draw your favourite toys. Write.

ball

21

Transport

1 **Look and write.**

rockets   boats   plane
bikes   trains   helicopters

four

three

one

two

six

five

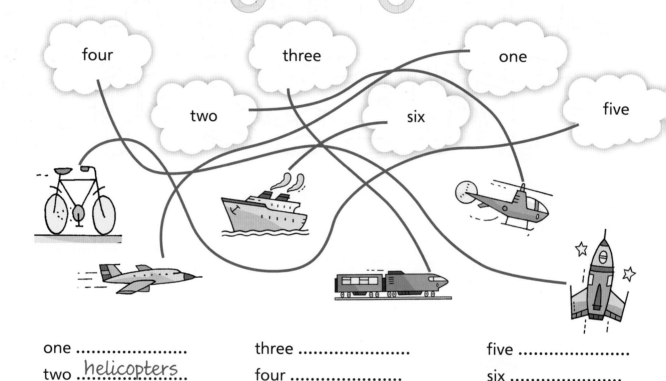

one ....

two .....**helicopters**.....

three ....

four ....

five ....

six ....

2 **Read, draw and colour.**

Colour the rocket orange.
Draw a red plane under the rocket.
Draw two blue bikes under the
plane.
Draw a green school bus next to
the bikes.

3 Look out of the window for five minutes and count.

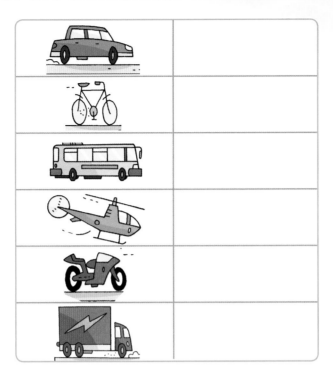

4 *Fun at home* Make a paper plane. Show your family. You need paper and your hands.

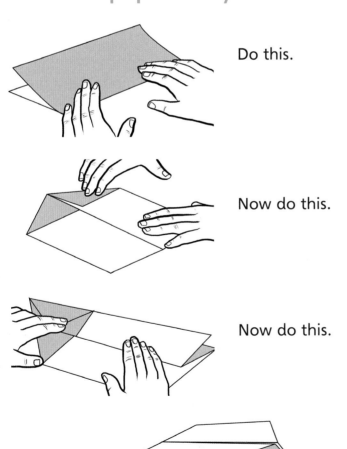

Do this.

Now do this.

Now do this.

Make your plane fly!

Numbers

1 **Look and write and colour.**

...........one.........
Colour it pink.

....
Colour them purple.

....
Colour them blue.

....
Colour them grey.

....
Colour them black.

....
Colour them brown.

....
Colour them green.

....
Colour them orange.

....
Colour them yellow.

....
Colour them green and white.

....
Colour them red.

....
Colour them blue and orange.

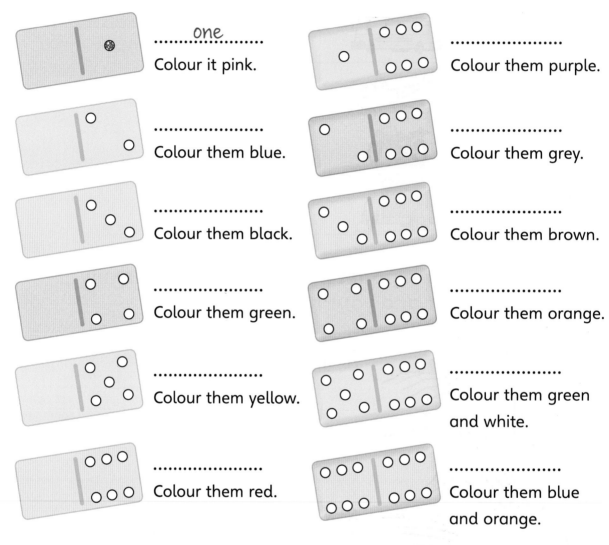

2 **Read and colour.**

Number thirteen is green.
Number fifteen is grey.
Number twenty is pink.
Number fourteen is orange.
Number eighteen is blue.
Number sixteen is red.
Number seventeen is yellow.
Number nineteen is purple.

13	14
15	16
17	18
19	20

3 Look at your bedroom. Count. Write.

Things	How many?

In my bedroom I have got

....

....

....

....

....

....

....

4 Colour. Look and tell your family.

I can see three brown cows.

25

Places

1 Write the names of the places.

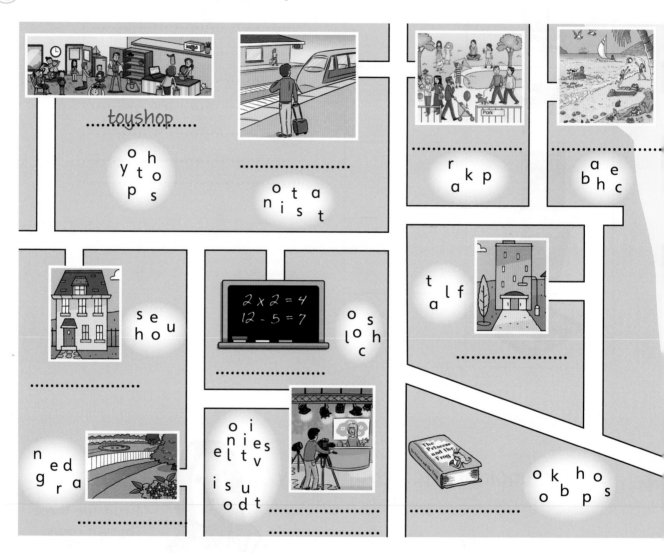

......toyshop......

o h
y t o
p s

....

o t a
n i s t

....

r
a k p

....

a e
b h c

s e u
h o

....

2 x 2 = 4
12 - 5 = 7

o s
l o c
c

....

t l f
a

....

n e d
g r a

....

o i
n i e s
e l t v
i s u
o d t

....

o k h o
o b p s

....

2 Lucy's day. Look at the things. Where is she going?

Write.

1 ......book — bookshop......
2 ....
3 ....
4 ....
5 ....

beach ~~bookshop~~ station
toy shop park

26

3 Write about your town.

Place	✓/ ✗ How many?

Place	✓/ ✗ How many?
$2 \times 2 = 4$ $12 - 5 = 7$	

In my town there are ....

There is a ....

There isn't a ....

There are lots of ....

There aren't any ....

....

....

4 Look at Ben's street.

bookshop   park

Draw your street and write what is in the street.

27

Time

1 Find words. Write.

afternoonbirthdayclockeveningmorningnightwatchyear

afternoon

....

....

....

....

....

....

....

2 Look, read and write.

have lessons   watch TV   go to school   have a bath   have dinner
have breakfast   go to sleep   ~~get up~~   ~~put on clothes~~   say goodbye   have lunch

In the morning, I ..get..
up and put on my
clothes. I have
breakfast. I go to
school.

In the afternoon, I ....

....

....

....

....

In the evening, I ....

....

....

....

....

At night, I ....

....

....

....

....

3 My day! This is Ben.

I like the afternoon. I play basketball with my friends.

What's your favourite time of day? Draw and write.

My name is ....
I like ....
I play ....
I go ....

4 Your day. Draw and tell your family.

morning

afternoon

evening

night

In the morning ....*I get up and have breakfast.*........... .
In the afternoon I ....
In the evening I ....
At night I ....

abc ✓

How do you spell the words?

 m _ _ _ _ _ _

 e _ _ _ _ _ _

The world around us

1 **Circle and write.**

....beach....

z	d	j	k	c	z	w	s	e	a
h	p	l	g	e	x	a	t	i	y
i	t	s	a	n	d	t	r	b	v
e	l	s	d	r	o	e	e	h	s
l	o	l	i	d	t	r	e	e	u
s	h	e	l	l	s	e	t	k	n
u	o	m	b	v	r	i	u	e	d
u	s	q	p	b	e	a	c	h	f

....

....

....

....

....

....

2 **Read, draw and colour.**

Colour the sun orange.
Draw three trees under the sun.
Draw two big fish in the sea, next to the boat.
Colour the fish pink.
Colour the sea blue.
Colour the man's hat red.
Colour the woman's hat green.
Colour the sand yellow.

3 Look and read. Write *True* or *False*.

Example It's a sunny day at the beach.

.........*True*.........

1 There's a monkey in the tree.

....

2 Two girls are playing with a ball.

....

3 A woman is sleeping under the tree.

....

4 Three birds are flying. ....

5 There is a cat in the boat. ....

6 There are two boats on the sea.

....

7 There are no shells on the beach.

....

4 **Fun at home** Look outside your window. What can you see? How many are there?

Things	How many? 0? 1? 2?
(tree)	1
(sun)	
(clouds)	
(houses)	
(boats)	
(sea)	

The author would like to thank all her friends and colleagues at IH Córdoba for their help and inspiration over the years.

The author and publisher would like to thank the ELT professionals who reviewed the material at different stages of development: Lisa McNamara, Spain; Sarah Moore, Italy; Duygu Ozkankilic, Turkey; Jessica Smith, Italy.

Freelance Editorial Services by Trish Burrow.

Design and typeset by Wild Apple Design.

Cover design and header artwork by Chris Saunders (Astound).

Sound recordings by Ian Harker and dsound recording studios, London.

The authors and publishers acknowledge the following sources of copyright material and are grateful for the permissions granted. While every effort has been made, it has not always been possible to identify the sources of all the material used, or to trace all copyright holders. If any omissions are brought to our notice, we will be happy to include the appropriate acknowledgements on reprinting and in the next update to the digital edition, as applicable.

The publishers are grateful to the following for permission to reproduce copyright photographs and material:

Key: L = Left, C = Centre, R = Right, T = Top, B = Below, B/G = Background

Laetitia Aynié (Sylvie Poggio Artists Agency) pp.10(T), 23(B), 26(B); Joanna Boccardo 28(B) afternoon, morning, night, evening; Adrian Bijoo (Advocate Art) pp. 6(B), 7(C), 15(C), 20(B), 21, 30(T) sand; Chris Embleton-Hall (Advocate Art) pp. 6(T), 8(T), 16(T), 31(T) street, water; Andrew Elkerton (Sylvie Poggio Artists Agency) pp. 2(T) (B), 3(B), 8(B), 13(B), 26(T) beach, blackboard, 30(T) beach; Clive Goodyer (Beehive Illustration) pp. 4, 6(C), 22(T), 23(T), 27(B), 28(T) birthday, watch, calendar; Andrew Hamilton (Elephant Shoes Ink Ltd) pp. 6(T), 25(T), 26(T) garden; Brett Hudson (Graham-Cameron Illustration) pp. 5, 7(B), 11(B), 15(B), 18, 26(T) book, 29(B); Kelly Kennedy (Sylvie Poggio Artists Agency) pp. 17 (BR); Nigel Kitching pp. 4, 14 (T), 17(BL), 19(B); Arpad Olbey (Beehive Illustration) pp. 3(C), 10(B), 25(B), 29 (T), (C), 30(B); Anthony Rule pp. 12(B), 26(T) toyshop; Pip Sampson pp. 14(B), 30(T) sea, tree, 31(B); Melanie Sharp (Sylvie Poggio Artists Agency) pp.13(B); Jo Taylor pp. 26(T) park; Theresa Tibbetts pp. 30(T) sun; Matt Ward (Beehive Illustration) pp. 14(B) garden, 20(T), 26(T) train station, television studio; Sue Woollatt (Graham-Cameron Illustration) pp. 11(T), 12(T), 22(B), 24.